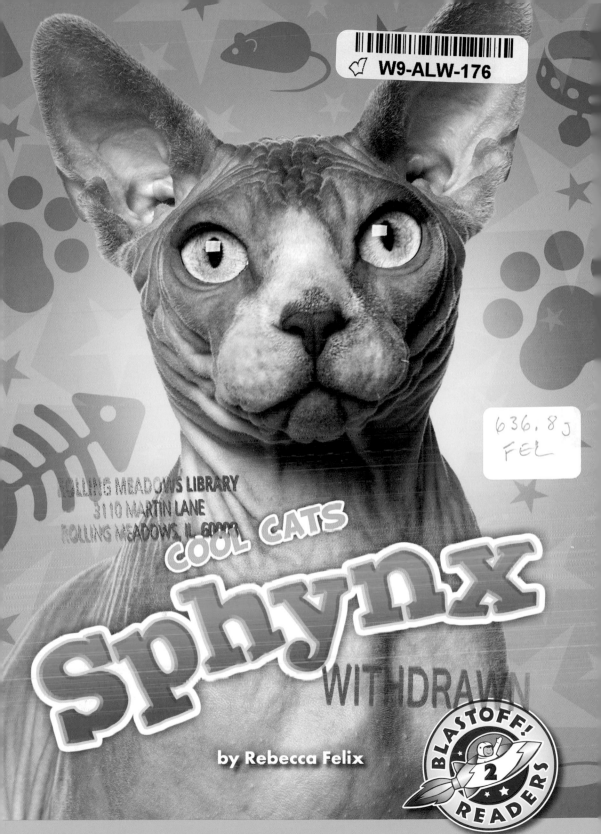

COOL CATS

Sphynx

by Rebecca Felix

BLASTOFF!
2
READERS

BELLWETHER MEDIA • MINNEAPOLIS, MN

Note to Librarians, Teachers, and Parents:

Blastoff! Readers are carefully developed by literacy experts and combine standards-based content with developmentally appropriate text.

Level 1 provides the most support through repetition of high-frequency words, light text, predictable sentence patterns, and strong visual support.

Level 2 offers early readers a bit more challenge through varied simple sentences, increased text load, and less repetition of high-frequency words.

Level 3 advances early-fluent readers toward fluency through increased text and concept load, less reliance on visuals, longer sentences, and more literary language.

Level 4 builds reading stamina by providing more text per page, increased use of punctuation, greater variation in sentence patterns, and increasingly challenging vocabulary.

Level 5 encourages children to move from "learning to read" to "reading to learn" by providing even more text, varied writing styles, and less familiar topics.

Whichever book is right for your reader, Blastoff! Readers are the perfect books to build confidence and encourage a love of reading that will last a lifetime!

This edition first published in 2016 by Bellwether Media, Inc.

No part of this publication may be reproduced in whole or in part without written permission of the publisher. For information regarding permission, write to Bellwether Media, Inc., Attention: Permissions Department, 5357 Penn Avenue South, Minneapolis, MN 55419.

Library of Congress Cataloging-in-Publication Data

Felix, Rebecca, 1984- author.
  Sphynx / by Rebecca Felix.
     pages cm. – (Blastoff! Readers. Cool Cats)
  Summary: "Relevant images match informative text in this introduction to sphynx cats. Intended for students in kindergarten through third grade"– Provided by publisher.
  Audience: Ages 5-8
  Audience: K to grade 3
  Includes bibliographical references and index.
  ISBN 978-1-62617-236-4 (hardcover: alk. paper)
  1. Sphynx cat–Juvenile literature. 2. Cat breeds–Juvenile literature. I. Title.
  SF449.S68F45 2016
  636.8–dc23
                              2015008701

Printed in the United States of America, North Mankato, MN.

Table of Contents

What Are Sphynx?   4
History of Sphynx   8
Wrinkly and Wide-eyed   12
Snuggly Showoffs   18
Glossary   22
To Learn More   23
Index   24

What Are Sphynx?

Sphynx are a **unique** cat **breed**.

The cats are almost entirely hairless!

Sphynx are famous for their soft, **wrinkled** skin.

They are also known
for their huge ears.

History of Sphynx

This breed began in Canada. A cat in Toronto gave birth to a special kitten in 1966.

The kitten was hairless! This was a natural **mutation**.

People **bred** more hairless cats. They named the cats after the Sphinx. It is a cat-like **sculpture** in Egypt.

Sphinx

Today, sphynx are bred around
North America and Europe.

Wrinkly and Wide-eyed

Sphynx have medium-sized bodies. They are covered in wrinkles.

They have large, firm bellies.
They always look as though
they just ate a big meal!

These cats have no fur. But they do have a layer of fuzz. Some have short hairs on their tails, toes, noses, or ears.

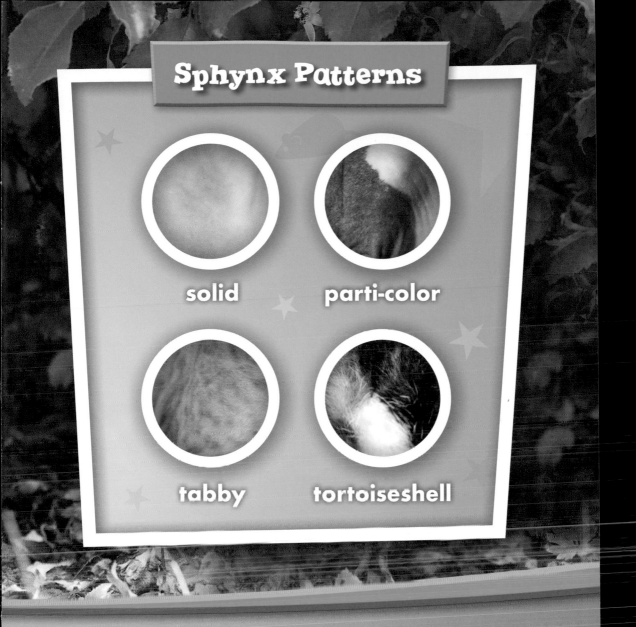

Sphynx Patterns

solid

parti-color

tabby

tortoiseshell

Their skin can be any **solid** color or **parti-color**. It may also be **tabby** or **tortoiseshell**.

Sphynx have short whiskers, or no whiskers at all! Their ears and eyes are big and wide.

Sphynx Profile

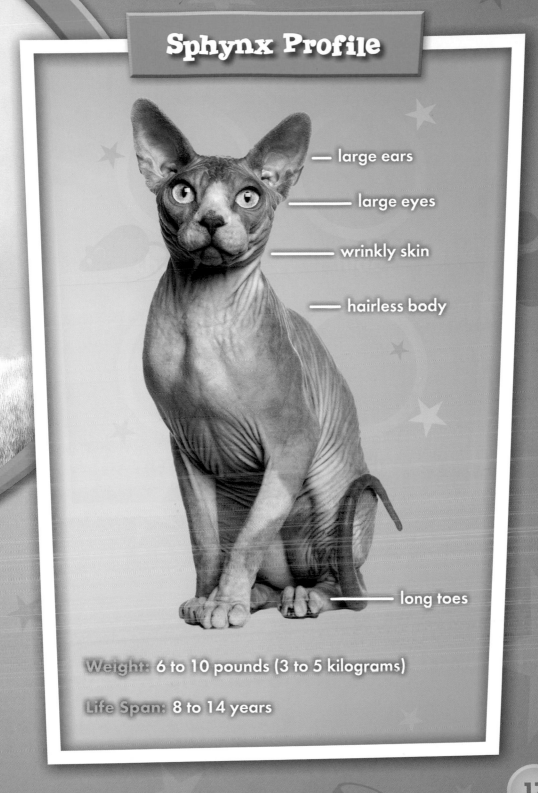

— large ears

— large eyes

— wrinkly skin

— hairless body

— long toes

Weight: 6 to 10 pounds (3 to 5 kilograms)

Life Span: 8 to 14 years

Snuggly Showoffs

Sphynx are playful cats.
They have a lot of energy.

They love to be the center of attention and often show off.

Sphynx are sometimes called "Velcro lap cats." They always want to sit on people's laps.

These cats curl up in other warm places, too. Many snuggle under blankets with their owners!

Glossary

bred—purposely mated two cats to make kittens with certain qualities

breed—a type of cat

mutation—a new form of something that has changed

parti-color—a pattern that is mainly one color, but with patches of one or more other colors

sculpture—an artwork that is carved

solid—one color

tabby—a pattern that has stripes, patches, or swirls of colors

tortoiseshell—a pattern of yellow, orange, and black with few or no patches of white

unique—one of a kind

wrinkled—covered in lines or folds in the skin

To Learn More

AT THE LIBRARY

Hengel, Katherine. *Smooth Sphynx*. Edina, Minn.: ABDO Pub., 2010.

Landau, Elaine. *Sphynx Are the Best!* Minneapolis, Minn.: Lerner, 2011.

Owen, Ruth. *Sphynx*. New York, N.Y.: PowerKids Press, 2014.

ON THE WEB

Learning more about sphynx is as easy as 1, 2, 3.

1. Go to www.factsurfer.com.

2. Enter "sphynx" into the search box.

3. Click the "Surf" button and you will see a list of related web sites.

With factsurfer.com, finding more information is just a click away.

Index

bellies, 13

bodies, 12, 17

bred, 10, 11

breed, 4, 8

Canada, 8

colors, 15

ears, 7, 14, 16, 17

Egypt, 10

energy, 18

Europe, 11

eyes, 16, 17

fuzz, 14

hairless, 5, 9, 10, 17

hairs, 14

life span, 17

mutation, 9

North America, 11

noses, 14

owners, 21

patterns, 15

show off, 19

size, 12, 17

skin, 6, 15, 17

snuggle, 21

Sphinx, 10

tails, 14

toes, 14, 17

Toronto, 8

Velcro lap cats, 20

whiskers, 16

wrinkled, 6, 12, 17

The images in this book are reproduced through the courtesy of: Eric Isselee, front cover, pp. 12, 15 (top left), 17; Indigo Fish, p. 4; Juniors Bildarchiv/ Superstock, p. 5; Tanee, p. 6; Jagodka, p. 7; Asichka, p. 9; Pius Lee, p. 10; dezi, pp. 11, 13; Labat-Rouquette/ Kimball Stock, p. 14, Kuchalkina Veronika, p. 15 (top right); Andrey_Kuzmin, p. 15 (bottom left); bonzodog, p. 15 (bottom right); Deposit Photos, p. 16; Ermolaev Alexander, p. 18 (top); Iriana Shiyan, p. 18 (bottom); Utekhina Anna, p. 19; Kekyalyaynen, p. 20; arttonick, p. 21 (top); MillaF, p. 21 (bottom).